HOW TO DRAW MANGA

David Antram

BOOK HOUSE

SALARIYA

Published in Great Britain in MMX by
Book House, an imprint of
The Salariya Book Company Ltd
25 Marlborough Place, Brighton BN1 1UB

3 5 7 9 8 6 4

Please visit our website at **www.book-house.co.uk**
or go to **www.salariya.com** for **free** electronic versions of:
You Wouldn't Want to be an Egyptian Mummy!
You Wouldn't Want to be a Roman Gladiator!
You Wouldn't Want to be a Polar Explorer!
You Wouldn't Want to sail on a 19th-Century
   Whaling Ship!

Author: **David Antram** was born in Brighton, England, in 1958. He studied at Eastbourne College of Art and then worked in advertising for fifteen years before becoming a full-time artist. He has illustrated many children's non-fiction books.

Editor: Rob Walker

PB ISBN: 978-1-907184-30-7

A CIP catalogue record for this book is available from the British Library.

Printed and bound in China.
Printed on paper from sustainable sources.
Reprinted in 2012.

WARNING: Fixatives should be used only under adult supervision.

PAPER FROM
SUSTAINABLE
FORESTS

Contents

Making a start

Learning to draw is about looking and seeing. Keep practising and get to know your subject. Use a sketchbook to make quick sketches. Start by doodling and experimenting with shapes and patterns. There are many ways to draw; this book shows one method. Visit art galleries, look at artists' drawings, see how friends draw, but above all, find your own way.

Use simple shapes to draw the figure in action.

Perspective

If you look at any object from different viewpoints, you will see that the part that is closest to you looks larger, and the part furthest away from you looks smaller. Drawing in perspective is a way of creating a feeling of space — of showing three dimensions on a flat surface.

The vanishing point (V.P.) is the place in a perspective drawing where parallel lines appear to meet. The position of the vanishing point depends on the viewer's eye level. Sometimes a low viewpoint can give your drawing added drama.

V.P.

V.P.

Two-point perspective drawing

Low eye level
(view from below)

Two-point perspective uses
two vanishing points: one for
lines running along the length
of the object, and one on
the opposite side for lines
running across the width of
the object.

V.P.

V.P.

Normal eye level

V.P.

V.P.

High eye level
(view from above)

V.P.

V.P.

V.P. = vanishing point

7

Drawing tools

ere are just a few of the many tools that you can use for drawing. Let your imagination go, and have fun experimenting with all the different marks you can make.

Pencil

Watercolour pencil

Charcoal pencil

Charcoal stick

Pastels

Finger painting

Black, grey and white pastel on grey sugar paper

Each grade of **pencil** makes a different mark, from fine, grey lines through to soft, black ones. Hard pencils are graded as H, 2H, 3H, 4H, 5H and 6H (the hardest). An HB pencil is ideal for general sketching. Soft pencils are graded from B, 2B, 3B, 4B, 5B to 6B (the softest and blackest).

Watercolour pencils come in many different colours and make a line similar to an HB pencil. But paint over your finished drawing with clean water, and the lines will soften and run.

It is less messy and easier to achieve a fine line with a **charcoal pencil** than a stick of charcoal. Create soft tones by smudging lines with your finger. **Ask an adult** to spray the drawing with fixative to prevent further smudging.

Pastels are brittle sticks of powdered colour. They blend and smudge easily and are ideal for quick sketches. Pastel drawings work well on textured, coloured paper. **Ask an adult** to spray your finished drawing with fixative.

Experiment with **finger painting**. Your fingerprints make exciting patterns and textures. Use your fingers to smudge soft pencil, charcoal and pastel lines.

Ballpoint pens are very useful for sketching and making notes. Make different tones by building up layers of shading.

A **mapping pen** has to be dipped into bottled ink to fill the nib. Different nib shapes make different marks. Try putting a diluted ink wash over parts of the finished drawing.

Draughtsmen's pens and specialist **art pens** can produce extremely fine lines and are ideal for creating surface texture. A variety of pen nibs are available which produce different widths of line.

Felt—tip pens are ideal for quick sketches. If the ink is not waterproof, try drawing on wet paper and see what happens.

Broad—nibbed **marker pens** make interesting lines and are good for large, bold sketches. Try using a black pen for the main sketch and a grey one to block in areas of shadow.

Paintbrushes are shaped differently to make different marks. Japanese brushes are soft and produce beautiful flowing lines. Large sable brushes are good for painting a wash over a line drawing. Fine brushes are good for drawing delicate lines.

Materials

Try using different types of drawing papers and materials. Experiment with charcoal, wax crayons and pastels. All pens, from felt-tips to ballpoints, will make interesting marks. Try drawing with pen and ink on wet paper.

Ink silhouette

Silhouette is a style of drawing which mainly uses solid black shapes.

Felt-tips come in a range of line widths. The wider pens are good for filling in large areas of flat tone.

10

Pencil drawings can include a vast amount of detail and tone. Try experimenting with the different grades of pencil to get a range of light and shade effects in your drawing.

Remember, the best equipment and materials will not necessarily make the best drawing — only practice will!

Hatching

Cross-hatching

Lines drawn in **ink** cannot be erased, so keep your ink drawings sketchy and less rigid. Don't worry about mistakes, as these can be lost in the drawing as it develops.

It can be tricky adding light and shade to a drawing with a pen. Use a solid layer of ink for the very darkest areas and cross-hatching (straight lines criss-crossing each other) for ordinary dark tones. Hatching (straight lines running parallel to each other) can be used for midtones.

11

Heads

Manga heads have a distinct style and shape. This is the basic shape of a head from the side and front views.

A simple side view of a head:

Start with a box to help you to proportion your drawing.

Draw an oval in the top two thirds of the box.

Add a line halfway up the box for the eye level.

Add a triangle shape for the eye.

Add the ear near the centre of the box.

Sketch in a triangle shape for the chin.

Sketch in the curve of the chin and add a neck.

Draw in the profile of the nose and mouth.

Draw in the arched eyebrows.

Add on the jagged shaped hair.

Add simple detail to the ear.

Complete the definition of the profile.

Finish any facial details.

A simple front view of a head:

First draw a large oval for the face. Draw two lines dividing the face horizontally and vertically through its centre. Add two small ovals on the horizontal line for the eyes.

On the vertical line mark in the position of the bottom of the nose and the mouth. Draw in the eyebrows. Add ears to the outside of the oval. Make the chin more angular by drawing a curved line from each ear to the centre of the oval.

Draw in the oversized shape of the eyes. Add the small nose and mouth. Draw in the hair using jagged lines and add shading to the eyes. Finish off by carefully removing the construction lines.

13

Expressions

Drawing different facial expressions is very important in manga. It's the way to show instantly what your character is thinking or feeling. Try drawing many different facial expressions.

Start by drawing an oval shape. Make it three dimensional with curved lines going through the centre.

Use these construction lines to add the basic details of the head (see page 13).

Using a mirror
Look at your own face in the mirror. By pulling different expressions, you will see how to draw these in your cartoons.

Add the mouth, eyebrows and shape of the nose.

Finish the drawing by adding hair and facial details, making the person look happy.

Now try drawing some different expressions. Here are a few ideas to get you started.

Laughing

Angry

Annoyed

Shocked

Surprised

Shouting

Hair

Manga characters generally have very stylised hair. Think about the situation the character you are drawing is in and make the hair fit the scene.

This character is drawn with five different hair situations.

Hair can be affected by action or environment. For example, if the character is running their hair may stream out behind them, or if it is windy the hair can be blown sideways.

16

Hair styles can help define your characters' personality. Here are a few different styles to try. What type of people do you think they belong to?

Samurai

The samurai warrior stands defiant, sword drawn and ready for battle.

Start by sketching these simple shapes.

Head

Draw an oval for the head.

Body

Draw two lines to indicate the position and angle of the shoulders and hips. Draw in a line for the spine.

Draw an oval for the body and smaller ovals for the hands.

Draw an oval for the hips.

Hand

Indicate the direction and length of the sword.

Sketch in the arms and legs using straight lines. Add dots to indicate the joints.

Now start to build up the basic shape and features of your figure.

Draw in the main shape of the body, using the ovals to guide you.

Draw in simple tube shapes for the arms and legs.

Feet

Sketch in simple shapes for the feet.

Drawing feet
These drawings show how the foot is built up from a simple shape to its finished form.

Now take your figure
a stage further.

Add details to the head,
defining the shape of the
nose, eye, ear and hair.

Start sketching in the
samurai's robes using
straight lines.

Complete the
details of the
face and hair.

Add a tied sash
to the front of
the robe.

Add the
sword
scabbard.

Add shading to
define the folds in
the robe.

Draw in the
shape of
the sword.

Complete the
sword with
single sharp
lines.

Start to build up the
shape of the feet.

Finish the
samurai's scabbard.

Finish the details of
the feet, adding sandals.

Carefully rub out any
unwanted construction
lines that remain.

19

Martial arts

Manga figures are often shown in action, performing martial arts moves.

Start by sketching these simple shapes for the figure.

Sketch an oval for the head.

Add an overlapping oval for the body and another for the hips.

Head

Body

Hips

Draw triangle shapes to position the feet.

Draw the limbs with straight lines.

Draw two lines to indicate the position and angle of the shoulders and hips. Draw in a line for the spine.

Indicate the joints with dots.

Legs

Feet

Sketch in the position of the facial features.

Add circles for the joints.

Using your construction lines as a guide, sketch the simple tube shapes for the arms and legs.

Draw in the shape of the fingers.

Add spiky hair and start to finish the face.

Draw in the shape of the clothes, making sure that they go around the body and flare out at the end of the limbs.

Draw the toes on the feet.

Draw a necklace swinging around the character's neck to add a sense of movement.

Complete the feet and ankles.

Complete the facial features.

Add shading and tone to the clothes.

Add creases to the cloth.

Dynamic backgrounds

Adding a dynamic background can give your drawing more impact. Try drawing straight lines coming out from the figure to give this kick more kick!

Remove any unwanted construction lines.

Warrior

This warrior is rushing into battle wielding a club. His action pose and sense of movement create a dynamic drawing.

Draw in different sized ovals for the head, body, hands and hips.

Club

Head

Draw limbs with straight lines.

Body

Hips

Only draw in one line for this leg because it is only the thigh that is visible in this pose.

Legs

Sketch in the club.

Indicate the joints with dots.

Feet

Using the construction lines as a guide, start drawing in the main shapes of the body.

Draw in circles for the joints.

Draw in tube shapes for the legs; remember that this pose will affect the leg length.

Draw in square shapes for the clenched fists.

22

Add details to the club.

Add more detail to the face.

Draw in the fingers.

Add the curved structure of the upper body and indicate the position of the belt.

Complete the gloved hand grasping the club.

Shade the bottom half of the legs.

Draw in the details of the clothing.

Add tone to emphasise the muscles.

Finish the belt.

Complete the drawing of the boots.

Shade areas like this, where light wouldn't reach.

Remove any unwanted construction lines.

23

Robot

This robot is built in a humanoid form and is ready to perform whatever task it is set.

Head

Arm

Hand

Body

Sketch in oval shapes for the hands.

Draw different sized ovals for the head, body and hips.

Add the visor of the robot's head.

Draw two lines to indicate the position and angle of the shoulders and hips. Draw in a line for the spine.

Draw simple lines for the limbs, adding dots at the joints.

Add the neck.

Start sketching in the robot's mechanical fingers.

Sketch in the shape of the arms and legs, adding circles for both elbows and knees.

Sketch in the shape of the feet.

Start to add the shape of the robot's limbs and mechanical joints.

The elbow joints are small cylinders.

Draw in the finger joints.

Make the tops of the legs thin.

Complete the head, adding a visor.

Finish the complicated hand parts.

Draw in the chest plate and shoulders with curved lines.

Add smooth shading to create the effect of shiny metal surfaces.

Remove any unwanted construction lines.

Light and shade
The amount and appearance of shading in a drawing depends on the strength and direction of a light source. Here we can see how the robot's arm casts different areas of shade depending on the direction of the light source.

25

Kimono girl

This girl is in a kneeling position and is dressed in a traditional oriental kimono. The draped folds of the costume can be challenging to draw.

Draw differently sized ovals, for the head, body and hips.

Head

Body

Draw two lines to indicate the position and angle of the shoulders and hips. Draw in a line for the spine.

Legs

As the figure is kneeling you only have to position the upper legs.

Sketch one hand going behind the head.

Position the facial features in the lower half of the head.

Add dots to position the joints.

Add both arms using the construction lines as a guide.

Place this hand on the figure's lap.

Start to draw the kimono using angular lines to create folds in the fabric.

Add the shape of the hair.

Draw in the sleeve, draping the cloth around the arms.

Add shading to the areas of draped folds where light wouldn't reach.

Draw in the fingers.

Complete the details of the face.

The legs are hidden under the kimono. Draw in the shape of the cloth around them.

Complete the flowing hair using jagged lines.

Remove any unwanted construction lines.

Finish the details of the kimono, adding shading to the folds.

27

Explosive action!

This character is being thrown through the air by an explosion. This pose captures a sense of action and excitement!

Hands

Arms

Sketch in ovals for the head, body, hips, hands and feet.

Body

Hips

Legs

Draw two lines to indicate the position and angle of the shoulders and hips.

Feet

Start to add the shape of the hands.

Draw straight lines with dots at the joints for each of the limbs.

Indicate the position of the facial features.

Draw in the shape of the arms using simple tube shapes. The construction lines will help you to position the limbs and joints correctly.

Add more detail to the shape of the feet.

Add the shape of the legs using simple tube shapes. The legs are different sizes due to the exaggerated pose and perspective.

Draw in the shape of the fingers.

Add the hair to the head. Make it look as if it has been flung upwards by the blast.

Start drawing in the clothes. Make sure they go around the body.

Indicate the finger joints.

Finish drawing in the shape of the shoes.

Draw curved lines with patches of tone for the smoke.

Draw in ragged and torn details to the clothing to add a sense of drama.

Add shading where light would not reach.

Remove any unwanted construction lines.

Draw straight lines coming from the explosion for added dramatic effect.

29

Glossary

Composition The positioning of a picture on the drawing paper.

Construction lines Guidelines used in the early stages of a drawing which are usually erased later.

Cross-hatching A series of criss-crossing lines used to add shade to a drawing.

Fixative A type of resin used to spray over a finished drawing to prevent smudging. **It should only be used by an adult.**

Hatching A series of parallel lines used to add shade to a drawing.

Light source The direction from which the light seems to come in a drawing.

Profile A view from the side, especially a side view of a person's head or face.

Reference Photographs or other images used to help produce a drawing, if drawing from life is not possible.

Silhouette A drawing that shows only a dark shape, like a shadow.

Three-dimensional Having an effect of depth, so as to look lifelike or real.

Vanishing point The place in a perspective drawing where parallel lines appear to meet.

Index